CREATIVE

OR

REACTIONARY

ELI HERNANDEZ

Copyright ©2022
All rights reserved. Written permission must be secured from the author to reproduce any part of the book.

Printed in the United States of America

ISBN: 9798375807096

10 9 8 7 6 5 4 3 2 1

EMPIRE PUBLISHING
www.empirebookpublishing.com

ADVANCE PRAISE

The ministry of Eli Hernandez has helped thousands of people through the years. It seemed that he could *see* things in the Spirit—and we wanted to know more about what he saw. This book opens those doors for us to gain Spiritual insight into things we have often wondered about. As I read this manuscript, I realized this book could be a "game changer" for many. The day I received and read it, I sent it to a man in my church that was going through the trial of his life. Upon reading it, his response was, "This reading really blessed me and gave me a whole new perspective." It transformed the way he was looking at his trial. Read it and pass it on to those in battle today to impart help and hope.

Pastor Randy Blizzard
Licensed Clinical Christian Counselor, Las Vegas, NV

Eli Hernandez walked in places few men have ever been. He spoke of some things he saw, but for the most part he kept those experiences to himself and did not reveal them to us. What he did was show us the pathway where we could enter into those places and have our own experiences with God. This book shows us how to move our attention away from the carnal world and its reactionary life and into the heavenly realm that is creative. Brother Eli Hernandez reveals to us the proper perspective we need to have throughout any difficult situation. This book will change your spiritual walk and help you keep your focus where it needs to be.

In remembrance of this great prophet of God,

Michael Mendenhall, M.B.A.
Pastor Soldotna Pentecostals, Soldotna Alaska/
Abba Father Christian fellowship, Kodiak Alaska

When you encounter a passionate person, their passion is contagious and stirs excitement in you. Brother Eli Hernandez was a man passionate about God and His Word. As a child, I remember him ministering at my home church. I was intrigued at how this gifted man of God shared the Word. He would walk through the aisles, ministering to the people with confidence, preaching the gospel to all of us—yet being sensitive enough to minister to individual members of the congregation.

Later in life, I had the privilege of presenting him to the congregation the Lord has called me to pastor. We were both older, but his ability to stir a passion remained. He was more than a traveling preacher—he was a man that loved God and was relatable, passionate, profound, personable, humble, and focused. He stirred people to love more, seek more, and live in the light. In life, his passionate delivery of the Word made you want to go deeper. This book is no different; may all who read it be encouraged to walk in the places God has called us to walk in.

Philip Spellman
Senior Pastor, Harrison Hills Church, Jewett, OH

As you read through *Creative or Reactionary* you will once again be challenged to think and feel in dimensions that we rarely access—though the author continually did. The spiritual concepts presented in this book turn our thinking on its head so that we can truly have a relationship with God that brings the creative into our life and ministry. As only Brother Eli Hernandez could do, he has shown us that, though hell is reactionary, Heaven is creative. It is time for the church to learn to access the creative of God in our lives.

Pastor Ryan Crossley
The Rock Church of Hollywood, Hollywood, Florida

The words that you will find written herein will enrich your life. *Creative or Reactionary* will impart to you spiritual insight and biblical principles that will revolutionize your prayer life. May you get into divine alignment as you read its pages. It is my privilege to recommend to you this book initially preached by my precious evangelist mentor. Thank you, Sister Hernandez and Sister Charity, for taking the time to transcribe this treasure, giving us an invaluable gift!

Evangelist Ethan Hagan
The Life Church of Kansas City

Creative or Reactionary is a book birthed out of a message preached by Prophet Eli Hernandez in California. I remember this message well, as I was present at that service. It was evident that the revelation coming forth was straight from the throne room.

As I read this book, I was thoroughly grateful that Sister Hernandez was obedient to prophetic command. It is obvious that this book is not just a book; rather, it is a prophetic utterance of instruction to the End Time church of today. Whatever stage in your journey with God you are currently in, you will want to read this word from God. It will change your perspective toward the spirit world and your part in it. A must read indeed!

Ezekiel Rodriguez
Senior Pastor, First Family Community Church,
National City, CA

Creative or Reactionary was a message preached at Impart Conference in 2018. As I listened, I found myself trying to pen every word spoken.

I am thankful Sister Hernandez listened to the prompting of the Spirit to pen the message into a book. I no longer have a few notes but rather all the revelations that were dropped that day.

The spiritual metamorphosis that began at that service has now processed into an ongoing change in my life. This book is not a sit through reading but a process of transformation. Read. Pray. Repent. Explore. Why? In order to fulfill His Will in this End Time harvest; we need to align ourselves to His creative thinking.

Dalila Rodriguez, M.A. Ed. Curriculum and Instruction
Teacher and licensed minister, National City, CA

I was privileged to have met and personally known the late Prophet Eli Hernandez. Having memorable trips overseas to the Philippines and Australia, seeing many miracles, and learning from this great man of God was truly life changing! He was a mentor and a friend.

I can clearly remember the night when he preached this revelation of God's creative power in one of the Impart Conferences that our church hosted, and I am very thankful that we are in an exciting journey of learning and exploring these "new" things that the Man of God spoke of and imparted to us.

This book will challenge your spiritual perception and even fine tune it, especially during challenging times. When facing difficulties, our natural inclination is to react; however, as you read this book, it will encourage you not to react but to perceive what the Creator, Jesus Christ, has released into your life. It will change you from simply being reactionary to thriving in the creative dimensions of God!

Pastor Nonoy Lachica
Spirit & Truth Lighthouse, Mission Viejo, CA

My dear friend, Eli Hernandez, was born for Kingdom Purpose. He was a warrior who encouraged his prayer team to fight from the vantage point of *"heavenly places in Christ Jesus."* This vantage point invited Brother Hernandez to see through the eyes of Jesus, giving Him revelation concerning the creative-reactionary response.

There is a growing hunger in people to receive wisdom and understanding. This is the hour of the Church—we need to hear the voice of God. I pray the message of *Creative or Reactionary* will reach into the deepest parts of the church and challenge us to move deeper into the Jesus Dimension.

This book is filled with life lessons, real-time experiences, and tremendous spiritual insight. *Creative or Reactionary* reveals the intense desire of the author to portray a concept that will challenge us to have a Kingdom perception when dealing with the enemy as God puts the creative in us for future encounters.

Thank you, Kathy and Charity Hernandez, for laboring to put this timeless message in writing. It is rich, insightful, and anointed-- words written with a powerful *creative* force.

May our response to whatever we encounter be the Creative Word of God and *not* the reactionary response of the enemy.

Donna Ten Eyck
Speaker, Prayer Coordinator, Office Administrator,
MS District UPCI

Table of Contents

ADVANCE PRAISE 1
FOREWORD 7
PREFACE 8
INTRODUCTION 11
CHAPTER 1 13
CHAPTER 2 17
CHAPTER 3 20
CHAPTER 4 25
CHAPTER 5 28
CHAPTER 6 33
CHAPTER 7 36
CHAPTER 8 41
CHAPTER 9 45
CHAPTER 10 48
CHAPTER 11 51
SPECIAL THANKS 55
ABOUT THE AUTHOR 57

FOREWORD

Eli Hernandez held a very special place in the Kingdom of God. His messages were informative concerning the operation of the Kingdom and its supernatural miracles, signs, and wonders. Along with these great revelations, there was impartation and knowledge when Brother Hernandez preached. Attending one of these special meetings, I heard the message *Creative or Reactionary*. I was taken aback by the deep revelation of the supernatural that was in this message. As I listened, the Lord spoke to me, "This is a message that will become a book upon which thousands shall receive revelations."

I highly recommend this book to be on the shelves, in the homes, and within the hearts of every saint of God. As you read this book, you shall forever receive new in-depth instruction in your walk with God to allow you to move from the earthly to the spiritual. It will unfold revelation about some of the secrets of your enemy that you battle daily and truths about how to take the high ground. This book will be worth every dollar you spend towards purchasing it.

Your servant,

Gordon Winslow, Sr.

PREFACE

It was a Thursday morning service in October of 2018; we excitedly gathered to hear a Word from the Lord. The Impart Conference, held at Spirit and Truth Lighthouse, in Mission Viejo, California, had grown in attendance from year to year. Hunger for God's spiritual movement had increased to the point where even a morning service in the middle of the work week yielded a full house!

That morning, as Evangelist Eli Hernandez preached this message, "Creative or Reactionary," the witness of God's Spirit in the sanctuary steadily increased. The power of God was great, and the heavenly atmosphere continued to intensify until the culmination of the altar call, where everyone present flooded the front of the building in prayer. We could feel the unified desire among us to follow God's ways, as that desire drew us all together in an outpouring of prayer. Many lives were changed and tremendously encouraged by this powerful message.

Rev. Gordon Winslow, the very next service, began to speak with a prophetic utterance. He announced that the message delivered by Eli Hernandez that morning, "...needs to be a book!" I took that to heart, wrote it down in my notes, and later asked for the audio recording of the message, "Creative or Reactionary." I kept it in a safe place, waiting for the unction from the Holy Ghost to begin transcribing this material into a book—all for the glory and honor of the Lord Jesus Christ.

Eighteen busy months passed, full of much traveling and ministry— with very few breaks. Suddenly, everything stopped abruptly, as the COVID-19 pandemic hit.

In March of 2020, Eli Hernandez was hospitalized (because of a high fever that would not break and increasing shortness of breath)—then the ventilator—then ICU—then an induced coma. After 45 days of isolation, Evangelist Eli Hernandez was victoriously whisked away up to Heaven, escorted by a great company of angels—no doubt hearing the words, "Well done, thou good and faithful servant." His work here on earth was complete. Now, we "...which are alive and remain..." must continue to follow the Lord's voice and the paths that He has set for each one of us to follow.

Upon the author's passing, the Lord clearly spoke to me, "Three books." The first one quickly materialized, as Rev. Adam Martinez came to me with the transcription of Eli Hernandez' lessons for Youth and Young Adults. We felt the confirmation from the Lord to publish the transcriptions, and in March of 2021, "Maintaining Divine Operation" was published. A few months later, "A World Beyond the Stars" was published. This book, written by Eli Hernandez, was in the editing process when he passed away.

I knew this third book was to be titled, "Creative or Reactionary." I must say, transcribing this material was not easy. It is heart-wrenching to hear the voice of a loved one who no longer inhabits the earth. But, with the help of the Lord and knowing this was His design—both by prophetic Word and by His Spirit in prayer—we have done our very best to represent this timely message in book form.

It is very interesting to note that, at one point in this book, the author states that he would be teaching these spiritual concepts "all over the world." Looking forward, I wonder where God will take these messages now that they are in writing. Is this a prophecy that is being fulfilled in a way that we could never have imagined? Our Lord tends to give us words and promises—and we hold on to them, excitedly awaiting their fulfillment. The crazy thing is that they almost always come to pass in a way we never would have imagined! It's always bigger, better, more heavenly, and beyond what we could ask or even think.

As the verse states in Ephesians 3:20-21 (KJV)
"Now unto him that is able to do exceeding abundantly above all that we ask or think, according to the power that worketh in us,

Unto him be glory in the church by Christ Jesus throughout all ages, world without end. Amen."

What a wonderful Savior our Lord Jesus is, full of wonder and might, who loves us and leads us into heavenly places. Unto Him be all Glory! Greater things are ours to explore—the Lord working with us, going before us, leading us closer to Him, and ultimately bringing us to the "...world without end."

Walk toward the light, delight in His ways, and may the Glory of God direct your steps. We pray this book will inspire you to seek the Lord daily, finding new revelations in Him; the Lord's Will be done here on earth, as it is in Heaven.

In His service,

Kathy Hernandez

INTRODUCTION

In Romans 1:11, Paul said, "That I may impart unto you some spiritual gift." He wrote those words while he was in prison, saying, "I desire to actually come and see you, that I may impart some spiritual gift."

Can you imagine still being in the "mode" of desiring to minister to others while you are in a prison?

Can you imagine the disposition a person would need to have so that while trapped in a prison house, he would still have a passion to minister to other people?

Most people, while in their "prison," have no desire to minister to anybody else; they want somebody to minister to them. But God said, "Paul, I'm going to teach you something completely different. In My Kingdom—regardless of what you're stuck in, what seems to have you trapped, what seems to 'wall 'you in, or what seems to bar you in—you're going to have an ability beyond the common and beyond normal. You're going to want to minister to people even while you are in a prison, left for dead, shipwrecked, talked about by your brothers, living with prisoners, and bound with chains on your way to go get judged in a common governor's house."

There is a dimension of God that has the ability to lift us to a place called the "supernatural." Receiving Heaven's supernatural assistance is the only way you can desire to impart unto others while you're stuck in a circumstance and in a prison.

God's purpose is that we would not be focused on our prison, but instead focused on our mission: "Go ye therefore into all the world, and preach the Gospel to every creature." God desires us to get to that place, where the things that are affecting and attacking our lives don't become the main product—or the main focus—of our minds. No matter what happens to us, our focus will remain on the Kingdom of Heaven and our purpose here on earth.

CHAPTER 1

I had a close friend who was possessed by seven demons. She was thrown to the ground by those spirits, white foam seeping from her dry mouth and tongue. I watched as men of God wrestled with her, earnestly praying for her to be delivered. She was probably around 5'2", but she threw those grown men like they were toys. I watched all of this at fifteen years old, quite astounded. After a season of time, they finally got the circumstance under control. My friend was delivered. She "broke through"—and she finally began peacefully speaking in tongues.

That's not hard for you to believe, is it?

Now, listen to this one. My wife and I had been praying for three to four hours in a church building in Wyoming. It had been three years since anyone had received the gift of the Holy Ghost there. The pastor was so discouraged; he was ready to leave.

As we prayed, the Holy Ghost began to move. Around the third hour of prayer, the power of God began to direct me and my wife; this was during the day, prior to the evening service, and God began to do miraculous things and speak prophetically.

When God begins to move like that, I certainly don't try to "figure it out." I try to absorb and ponder.

When God begins to move in supernatural veins, do not try to figure out what's happening— take it in and absorb what is happening because God is actually building layers into you that will be "un-layered" (uncovered or brought to the forefront) down the road, so He can use them. You see, Brother Cole always told me, "Son, you have to remember that some things are taught but some things are caught."

Take note. When you are in environments where the Spirit of God is moving, don't look at the size of the crowd. Don't measure the movement based on what you think you see but measure it by what's coming upon you because God is loosing layers upon you. Some of those layers won't be used for years; some of those layers will be put into you, and ten years down the road, God will open a layer. It is what's in your spirit, and God is putting it there for a time. He must bypass the brain because if God were to explain it to us within our brains, some stuff we just wouldn't receive!

For example, if God would have told me that I was going to go to Ethiopia and preach in front of 300,000 to 500,000 Ethiopians ten years before it happened, I would not have believed it. So, God just bypassed my brain, put it into my spirit, and gave me a dream. (It wasn't pizza.)

Ten years after that dream, I stood in front of a crowd in Ethiopia. When I stepped up to the pulpit and saw the people, then I remembered the dream– and God instantly connected ten years and said, "Remember? This is that moment I put in you ten years ago." God put the layer somewhere back in my spirit all those years ago to uncover it in His perfect timing.

We need to get accustomed to these things. There is something changing in the atmospheric timeline of God.

Previously, the times and seasons were not aligned to write about these things. ("To every thing there is a season, and a time to every purpose under the heaven:" Ecclesiastes 3:1) But God has done something since September 24, 2018. God has done something to me and for me and has begun to talk to me, releasing things that have been on hold for a season. In fact, it has already changed, and I think it is imperative we quickly align with what God has changed.

Back to our prayer meeting in Wyoming. We had been praying for hours. I was sitting in an aisle, and suddenly, I felt a drop on my arm. I had a short-sleeved shirt on. I looked up at the ceiling and then I looked down at my arm. There was a drop of blood on my forearm.

My natural mind said, "There are hydraulic lines in the church. What are hydraulic lines doing in the church?"

My spiritual being said, "What are you talking about? You're in the presence of God!"

Then I realized, "This is a drop of blood— from God!"

After reading about this event, what does your brain do?

Some of you, readers, are trying to calculate this situation. You didn't have to do that when I talked about devils; you only had to do that when I talked about supernatural movement in heavenly places. It's not because you're doubting, but because that's the way we've been trained. We've been trained to accept reactionary speech but haven't been trained to accept creative speech.

The Lord spoke to me and said, "Creative. Reactionary. Which are you?"

I said, "You tell me. You created me." When God asks a question, it is not as if He doesn't know the answer. When God asks me a question, I begin pondering. I'm not ignorant enough to think God doesn't know the answer. He's asking because He is trying to probe something out of me. He's trying to get something from me, to get me to admit or come face to face with something.

Why would God want to do that? Because He wants to transform the way we think. God never asks a question just because He wants to give us an answer. He asks a question to change our mindset on a particular subject because it is not yet fully changed into what He wants it to be.

If God ever asks you a question, don't just think He wants to have a nice conversation with you. The reason for that approach is because He is about to transform something in your life. It's like when He asked Ezekiel a question in Ezekiel 37:3, "Can these bones live?"

God wasn't asking him for a "yes" or "no" answer; rather, He was trying to create a platform because of what He was about to transform. God was about to make those bones come together and skin come over those bones. He was about to tell Ezekiel, "Speak to the wind!" Ezekiel was about to watch the creative take place, and for the creative to take place, God needs humanity's "buy-in." God can do the creative without us, but He doesn't want to. God wants us to have a "buy-in," so we become participants in the creative because God is creative.

On the other hand, hell cannot create anything. Hell is not a creator, nor does it have the ability to be able to create. Hell is reactionary. So, if we always function based on reaction, we will never step into the creative. God is trying to get His church to shift away from being so attentive to what's attacking us and to become more attentive to what He is creating for us.

I want to open some understanding here: everything that hell does is a reaction to what God has released creatively. So, when we function off an attack, how much of God do we actually see? When we are focused on the attack of the enemy, how much are we missing?

God has given me little excerpts of this along the way. He gives me glimpses because He's trying to train me. This concept was not taught when I was young. Back then, we were barely learning about the gift of faith and there was very little teaching about mass-miracles. There were very few men teaching on miraculous events, such as 100,000 people receiving the gift of the Holy Ghost in one service. Acts 2 principles were rarely talked about. Meanwhile, God was trying to teach us about the principles in Acts 16 and 19, where a handkerchief would be sent and somebody would get healed, or demons would leave, or an entire city would place their attention on God.

CHAPTER 2

Creative! What if God could take the attention of the church and put it where Paul said to put it. In Ephesians 2:6, Paul wrote "…and made us sit together in heavenly places in Christ Jesus…"

Paul did "sit in heavenly places." When you are in heavenly places, you don't have "hell" discussions. When you are in heavenly places, you are having angelic, creative, dominion, and miraculous conversations.

The majority of what Paul wrote was inscribed while he was in prison! One way to have heavenly conversations in a prison house is by singing praises unto God. When Paul and Silas were in the jail and began to sing heavenly praises, God worked the miraculous by automation, not by petition.

Petition gets you a response from God—but think about most petitions. Most petitions are on the preface of reaction, as in: "God, this person got attacked! They need deliverance," or, "God, this person has a baby who is on the verge of dying."

Think about this: God stretched a man's leg out in 40 minutes at the Azusa Street revival from the knee to the foot—which means God created a new foot. Those around the man told him, "God can not heal you if you believe you need that prosthesis—so take it off!" They took it off and prayed for him. He went backwards on the floor and was passed out for 40-45 minutes. After he got up, he looked down. God had recreated the rest of his leg and a brand-new foot. I thought, "Wait a minute. How do you get into that?" Then, it occurred to me. The man was asleep when the miracle happened, which means he could not "get in the way."

That's why God put Peter to sleep and gave him a dream—gave him a vision. Even while sleeping, he had an argument with God about it. Peter argued with God about going to the Gentiles in Acts 10—and he was asleep! Since he was sleeping, his present thinking—his frontal lobe—was shut down. This is partially because the frontal cortex remains relatively calm and doesn't activate during REM sleep. That means Peter argued with God in his subconscious mind—that was his cultural state.

The subconscious is developed during the first five to ten years of our lives and wraps itself around how we were each raised as a child. That cultural state includes the way we eat, the way we live, the words we hear, the approaches we have developed, and how we deal with things. We have all this training during our formative years, day after day, year after year, that contributes to the subconscious mind. This foundation is established from a very young age and must be reformed when we are saved—especially if we had a bad upbringing. Even if we had a good upbringing, it still needs to be reformed since most families don't raise their children thinking creatively; instead, they raise them thinking *reactionarily*.

Peter was a Jew. He was not supposed to be fraternizing with those who were not Jews. He should not have even been in the house of Simon the Tanner (a trade that was considered unclean by the Jews of his day).

Nevertheless, he was in the house of the tanner, which was already a struggle. And it wasn't just that, Peter now had seen a vision where God said, "You're going to the Gentiles," so Peter argued with God out of his cultural state. God was not trying to simply "bless" him; God was trying to transform him. It was as if God said, "I want to get into your subconscious mind. If I can have a miraculous thing happen in your subconscious mind and transform you there, you will not only reach the Gentiles and have an unprecedented revival, but when you are near death, you won't even mind getting crucified upside down because I'm going to change you from your subculture. I'm going to change everything about you—but I'm going to have to start in your dreams and your visions."

Why do you think God said, "And it shall come to pass in the last days, saith God, I will pour out of my Spirit upon all flesh: and your sons and your daughters shall prophesy, and your young men shall see visions, and your old men shall dream dreams" (Acts 2:17). Dreams and visions are mentioned here because the Lord said, "It's the only state I can operate in to get ahold of you, where your will isn't wrestling with me at its full capacity. You still have a will, but it's not wrestling in the frontal lobe state. Instead, it's wrestling in the subconscious state."

Creative Works. How do we get our brains, spirits, and minds to start thinking creatively—not creatively as in "ideas," but creatively as in "God-function"—in a supernatural realm, where heavenly things become commonplace? Paul referenced, "sitting in heavenly places." Sitting has to do with staying a while. The Bible didn't say Paul visited heavenly places; the Bible says he sat there. Ephesians 2:6 reads, "…and made us sit together in heavenly places in Christ Jesus…" That's the difference between visiting and dwelling.

This is similar to what the Bible says about dwelling in unity. Most of our churches don't dwell in unity, as far as "church to church." We visit unity, specifically at conferences, but we don't really dwell in unity. Dwelling in unity is hard work! How often does a church reach out to another church simply to fellowship (not because there is an event planned)? Let's just be honest: we don't because we don't have a culture like that. We didn't create a culture like that. So, God is trying to help the church to change the spiritual culture so that our culture automatically accommodates itself to heavenly things instead of hell attacks.

CHAPTER 3

Let's think about what hell really is: it's a distraction on steroids. God is operating at a much higher level. We know that the opposite of God is not the devil. There is no opposite of God. He is God. There is just God—that's it. He is all by Himself. You can talk about God's thousands of attributes for the next hour to three hours, but God is just God! So, why should the reactionary part of hell's actions be the attention of the church? It shouldn't. We should be able to step into God moments and not bring up hell moments. But every Pastor can tell you that many prayer requests are not based on what God said. Instead, they are based on what got attacked. We know this because most people, after they get attacked, go to God and cry, "Lord, please help me" instead of going to God and saying, "I got attacked. What did you create?"

Or, "I got hit. What did you release?"

Or, "My wife just got sick. What just got loosed out of Heaven?"

Or, "Hell raised up its head. Lord, what did You speak into the atmosphere? Because You are creative—but hell is reactionary."

If the devil is reactionary, that means he has got to be reacting to something. And if he's reacting to something, what is it? What is that "something" from heaven that I need to get a hold of. So, Lord, I'm advancing to heavenly places. I want to sit up here. I want to "hang-out" up here. I want to dwell with you and talk to you up here. I want to visit with you! I want to know what the mind of God is and what the mind of the Spirit is. I want to understand what the Christ operation of the Kingdom is at this moment. Lord, what are you creating that I didn't catch? I'm sorry that hell "caught it" before I did.

What if we could get to the place where we hear the creative Word of God before the enemy does? Let us pause and think about this concept. Where does the enemy dwell? Ephesians chapter 2 tells us that the enemy dwells in the mid-heaven. He is the prince and the power of the air, which is the second heaven. Paul said there is a third heaven; so, there obviously must be a second, and there must be a first. We live in the first heaven, and satan lives in the middle of nothing. Air is nothing. He is the owner of nothing. He doesn't own land, and he doesn't own heaven space. So, he doesn't own anything.

And you're afraid of some devil that's "renting?"

Satan has no dominion; therefore, he has no sword, no shield, and no helmet. He has no breastplate, no girding of the loins, and no "shodding" of the feet. We often get very excited about the devil having nothing. How excited do we get knowing God has everything?

We all know it's hard to keep that concept when you're under attack. This is why you need to pray through your emotional state because the emotional state is what gets attacked. It is the weakest state of humanity.

The devil is a "bully." He picks on the weakest state of humanity to keep us there, so we approach God in our weakest state. Faith is the strongest state of humanity. If hell keeps us in our weakest state through our emotions, we will never get to our strongest state. And the only way for the fear of the Lord to work through faith in us, is if we can get past the weakest state. So, how do we get there? We must pray our way to that place of faith and pray through to our strongest state.

That is why, when people are acting foolish in your church, you feel like telling them, "Why don't you just go pray through?" What we are really saying is, "Get past your emotional state." If you can get past your emotional state, you will start to see more clearly. If we tell someone to "settle down," we are really saying, "Look, you got attacked at your emotional state. Don't approach God that way because you're approaching Him at your most feeble point. Pray through!"

How do we do that? Repent.

The quickest way to overcome an emotional state attack is to repent because hell has no defense mechanism against repentance. That's why repentance is the key; it is the introduction to the Kingdom and salvation. This is why John the Baptist came preaching repentance before Jesus showed up. And that's why Isaiah prophesied about it 750 years before it was manifested in the flesh through Jesus Christ.

Repentance unlocks Heaven.

When Jesus was baptized by John in the baptism of repentance, the Bible says, "the heavens opened." When I repent, hell backs up. When hell backs up, Heaven opens up. When Heaven opens up, I am advancing toward heavenly places!

However, it might take us a while to reach heavenly places; for instance, we might need to repent for an hour because we are disconnecting from an attack. We do not always repent just because we did something wrong, although that should be the initial reason why we repent. But, to only repent when we do something wrong is another "misnomer of hell." That idea is not a "God-concept," but a "hell-concept." Repentance is originally and initially intended for connection with God. That's how people get to God—they must repent!

"Repent and be baptized, every one of you, in the name of Jesus Christ for the remission of sins, and ye shall receive the gift of the Holy Ghost" (Acts 2:38).

Let me test your mind with a brief example below:

If somebody comes to the altar and shouts, "I REPENT!" What do you think?

Do you think, "Wow, they're accessing Heaven"?

No. Instead, your brain automatically diverts to the initial thought, "What did they do wrong?" This is because we've learned the introductory benefit of repentance. Paul said, "I die daily," and if we assess this statement as meaning only repentance from mistakes, then it would have to mean that Paul sinned every night. We know that's not true. God used him to write multiple books in the New Testament! Do you think he struggled every night, so he repented every morning? I don't think we would believe that.

Rather, Paul is saying, "Look, I found a key!" According to the seven churches of Asia, it's the key of the church of Philadelphia. What did they have? The key of David. David was best known for repenting. He knew repentance better than he knew singing. Singing will not get you access to Heaven but repentance will.

When David came to God amid his atrocities, he knew, "A broken and a contrite spirit Thou wilt not despise." So, he repented. He understood, this is a key component in the Kingdom of Heaven– not because of what it removes but because of what it unlocks.

Here is an exercise that might help change your thinking. Repentance, initially, is about what it removes. But after that, it is for what it unlocks. If you study the history of Genesis to Malachi, you'll notice, in those 4,000 years, there was a closed Heaven. There was not an open Heaven. There were windows: Noah had a window, and Malachi had windows. Ezekiel had an out of body experience and entered into the Heavens once, but that was in a spiritual moment. There was not an existent "open Heaven." But when Jesus got baptized by John in Mark chapter 1, the Bible says, "The Heavens opened!"

Think for a moment with me. Jesus was perfect. He had no sin. So, what was He trying to teach us? When we are consumed in repentance, it detaches hell from us and unlocks Heaven for us. Here is the key: God is moving us from the reactionary state to the creative state. According to the book of Luke, there is joy in front of the angels when one sinner repents. It is the same terminology that is used in Luke 10:21, where Jesus had joy when the seventy-two went out in pairs. They came back and said, "Wow! The devils are subject unto us!" We often focus on this same thought process, even today. But, Jesus said, "Don't get caught up with that. Don't rejoice that hell is submitted to My authority; instead, get your mind on celestial things. Celebrate that your name is written in the Lamb's Book of Life."

Do you know what Jesus was trying to tell them? "Set your affection on things above, not on things on the earth" (Colossians 3:2). Get your mind on celestial thinking. The Lord has creative treasures that He wants to give His Church.

CHAPTER 4

If the only approach we have is from hell's reaction, how can God give us a creative Heaven? How can the Lord put creative seeds in a negative-natured approach? It's amazing–I can't wrap my mind around it; how could a person be negative with all the positive cells our bodies have? I can't figure that one out. We have positive cells in us. By nature of our creation, we are supposed to be positive, yet people come out with negative thought processes. How is that possible? It's what they are focused on. As my mother used to say, "Dime con quién andas y te digo quién eres."

Translated from Spanish to English, that means, "Tell me who you run with, and I'll tell you who you are." If I am always running with the attack, then I'm going to be a devil chaser.

I don't need to chase devils. If devils are bothering you, then pull out your wallet. Give an offering. The Bible says in Malachi that if we pay our tithes and offerings, He will rebuke the devourer for our sakes. So, if the devil is attacking you, pull out your wallet and say, "I dare ya."

That's what I do. I say, "You're going to come to my house? I'm not going to waste my time with you. What do you want me to give, devil? Do you want me to give one thousand, five thousand, ten thousand?"

I've got a "hit job." I say, "Lord, just send one of those small angels for me, would you? Because this nuisance is trying to take my time. He's reacting to something that you loosed out of Heaven, and I don't want to respond based on a reaction. I want to respond based on the creative."

John 1:3 says, "ALL THINGS were made by Him, and without Him was not anything made that was made. In Him was life…" So, every time God looses something creative, it has life built into it. Every time the devil reacts, there is death built into it. That's because he has come to steal, kill, and destroy. So, his reaction is for the purpose of us looking at what is dying, not what is being created. The devil's whole purpose is for us to focus on, "I'm going to lose this. This is going to die. This is going to fail. Oh God, HELP!"

Wait a minute. There's already life in the atmosphere if hell has responded to a creative Word, so I've got to look for life! I'm not looking for life that fixes my small stuff; I'm looking for life that consumes my entire world. Because, if the "creative" can get in me, what can it produce? What can it multiply? God is not just in the business of giving you a miracle, God is in the business of giving us multiplication.

That's why, every time prophecy comes forth—a Word comes forth—it's not just God prophesying or loosing a miracle in your life, He is actually loosing multiplication. For instance, when I was about 28 years old, I used to deliver five gallon jugs of water. This was before I started evangelizing in 1989. One day, a whole rack of those bottles, stacked seven high and six wide, fell on my back! My manager screamed as they toppled over, and I jumped out, trying to miss it. The top two bottles clipped my lower back, and it just messed me up. They tried to send me to therapy and told me that I was going to have to stay in therapy for months, but I was supposed to start evangelizing full time in three months. I thought, "God, if I end up staying in therapy, I'm not evangelizing—and I'm not evangelizing like this. I'm not doing it. I'm just not!"

Now, I don't speak to God like that all the time, but this one time, I thought, "God, I'm not going out there as a cripple. You didn't send me out there to evangelize as a cripple, and I feel like a cripple right now." I couldn't even walk or dress myself. That's how bad it was.

I went to minister at a revival around November that year, prior to us "hitting the road" full-time. I decided, "God, I'm not going to let this man of God down." So, I got to the house the pastor put us in, and my wife had to help me hobble to the room.

I was like a baby (men don't handle pain well). My wife had to help me get dressed. She would then help me over to the church, and I'd lay on the floor praying for the service and for God to move. After prayer, she would help me "hobble" back, and we'd grab something to eat. I'd lay down for a while in the evangelist's quarters before she would have to dress me for church. I arrived at service that night and soon it was time for the preaching to begin. I hit the pulpit and suddenly felt NO PAIN!

I felt like preaching for days back then because it was the only time I had relief. We saw people get healed! I saw miracles, signs, and wonders. I would be running, jumping, and moving during the preaching, and as soon as I was done preaching, I would be back in that crippled state. And I said, "God, whatever you're teaching me, can I get the Cliff Notes? Because I'd like to get through this a little quicker."

I lived like that the entire two-week revival. At the end of those weeks, God finally said, "OK, now you're ready." And it just lifted! But watch what happened: when God healed me, He didn't just heal me so I could go shouting, He healed me so, over the next 29 years, I would see hundreds of thousands of backs healed—across 55 countries! I didn't know then what the purpose was, but I understand it now.

Here's the reason hell is so reactionary: the devil knows if God starts doing the creative, it's not just for you. Rather, it's for everything you're going to touch, it's for everything you're going to speak, it's for everything you're going to have faith for, and it's for everything that's coming in your path.

Take a moment and lift your hands. Lift up your voice and allow God to plant something into your spirit as you entertain His presence.

When you are ready, continue to the next chapter.

CHAPTER 5

"In Him was life and the life was the light of men. And the light shineth in darkness and the darkness comprehended it not" (John 1:4-5).

Later on, Jesus makes this statement:

"And this is the condemnation, that light is come into the world, and men loved darkness rather than light, because their deeds were evil" (John 3:19).

The verse says that they loved darkness rather than light, for their deeds were evil.

This scripture doesn't have to do with bad habits and sin you can't get rid of. It has to do with a mindset and a presentation of your source. In the verse that commands us to set no wicked thing before our eyes, the word "evil" is used. That verse isn't talking about not having any evil thing set before you, as in a television. Instead, that verse is talking about the presentation of the Body of Christ, representing the King. Our representation to the world is not supposed to have an evil appearance. In other words, when the world looks at us, they shouldn't say, "Wow, you've got a poor king. He doesn't take care of you."

"Why are you sad? You must have a bad king!"

"Why are you depressed? You have a bad king."

"Why are you worried? Why are you stressed? Why are you overwhelmed?"

When we go out there, the King wants the best presentation of His Kingdom to be in the face of the world. That way, when the world looks at us, they say, "Wow, where have you been?"

And we can respond, "I've been in heavenly places."

When they say, "Wow, who have you been building a relationship with?"

We can say, "Jesus Christ is my King."

"Wow, how could you be going through that with such peace in your heart?"

"Because I have the 'peace-speaker' with me."

"How do you always have peace in your home?"

"Because He is the Prince of Peace!"

It's about presentation. The Lord said, "What happened to My people in the church who got so consumed with darkness that their presentation went bad?"

The Bible says, "…men loved darkness…". To love something, one needs to build a relationship with it. Those who became consumed ended up building a relationship with what was attacking them instead of what was saving them. The only conversations they had were about the reactionary.

Think about it. Suppose you go to your prayer room—hopefully you have a prayer room somewhere—or to an altar. If all you talk about is what is wrong, what is your presentation going to be? Your presentation will be negative because it's petition based. It is "earth-tied" instead of "Heaven-tied."

I did something a long time ago. I don't always do this, but every now and then, I will be reminded of it, and I will do it. It's the Lord's Prayer. I don't just go through it systematically. I was examining the part that says, "Thy Kingdom come, thy will be done in earth…" and the next line caught my attention: "As it is in Heaven." That turned into a question for me. I started saying, "Lord, let's skip all the preliminary stuff. How is it in Heaven right now? What's going on in Heaven? What are you saying in

Heaven? Can I get close? Can I peek into the general session this morning? What are you up to, God, that has caused hell to be so stirred up—so much so that all the people in the hotel (except me) couldn't sleep?" When others can't get to sleep, I just tell the devil what Evangelist Smith Wigglesworth did: he looked at the devil that walked in his room and said, "Oh, it's just you? I'm going to bed."

That's really how we ought to be. I'm taken aback by preachers who use the ladder of emotion to stimulate the crowd. They tell a story about how God conquered an evil spirit, or something of that nature, and use it to excite the people. Yet, they don't really tell about the God-dimension which caused the victory in the first place.

I was determined to get beyond that demonic focus because I was raised around that—all my life. I watched the wrestling of spirits, and I watched spirits attack.

You must realize that the devil can't graduate above flesh. His highest domain is flesh! He cannot rise above it. We've been made a little lower than the angels. Demons can't rise to the dimension of angels because they were cast out of that dimension. Lucifer and his angels have fallen, and they can't rise back to that level. Our highest dimension is the throne—God. Think about the contrast of that. There is no comparison! And so, our whole perception needs to have a transformation so that our focus is not darkness. Our focus should be: if there is darkness, what is it responding to?

All things were created in the atmosphere of faith. Nothing was created in the chamber of fear. When fear begins to work, it becomes difficult for faith to plant itself in "fear-soil." Fear is the operation of hell, constantly trying to speak to you, attack you, get your attention, and keep you attentive to the darkness. So, if your soil is always based on condition and fear, you're missing a whole lot of what God has already released in the atmosphere.

The fear of the Lord has a lot built into it. It has extended the days of man's life and has health built into it. It has peace built into it as well. There are multiple "fear of the Lord" phrases which go from the Old Testament into the New Testament, and through four dimensions of the apostolic, Book of Acts church. (That's a whole study in itself–and a wonderful study at that!) Studying this makes you realize: fear from the enemy is for the purpose of taking away a celestial dimension that is established through the fear of the Lord. The fear of the Lord is the beginning of Wisdom. If you go back to that contrast, that is the foundation for creative, miraculous things. Wisdom spoke as an entity when she said, "I was THERE...when the foundations of the worlds were framed. I was THERE when the fountains of the deep came forth." Wisdom is speaking like an entity, and God said, "I obtained Wisdom." And He used it in the days of creation.

So, God takes Wisdom as an entity, uses it as a component, and looses creative works upon the earth. It is no wonder that hell uses fear. It's trying to remove the dimensions of the fear of the Lord because those dimensions are creative.

You see, God gets the church back to the fear of the Lord in Acts 2:42-43 when "fear came upon the people" after they were filled with the Holy Ghost and began to speak in tongues and were baptized in Jesus' Name. When the church was born, the first act of restoration was the fear of the Lord. God had to restore the fear of the Lord, so the creative works could start working once again. That's why, after the fear of the Lord fell on them, the apostles did miracles. The same thing happened in Acts chapter 5, Acts chapter 9, and in Paul's description of using a handkerchief in Acts chapter 19. But, the four dimensions of the fear of the Lord is a graduation. God keeps bringing the church higher because it has separated itself from hell's attacks. That way, hell is not our focus. Heaven is our focus. Creative works are our focus. And then, the supernatural can easily flow!

Listen to this theological summary covering a scientific perspective on miracles. It simply states:

Science does not disprove Biblical miracles. Science depends upon observation and replication. Miracles...are by their very nature unprecedented events. No one can replicate these events in a laboratory. Hence, science simply cannot be judge and jury as to whether or not these events occurred. The scientific method is useful for studying nature, but not 'super-nature' (Rhodes, par. 1).

"Oh, the depth of the riches both of the wisdom and knowledge of God. How unsearchable are His judgements, and His ways past finding out. For who hath known the mind of the Lord, or who hath been His counselor?" (Romans 11:33-34)

I asked the Lord, "So, since there are obviously God-ways that are not natural to my mindset, here is what I'm asking you to help me accomplish until the day I die. Every day, give me a little nugget or a little turn in the road to help my brain to detach itself from the cyclic pattern of the natural man."

The natural man is sin-natured, and sin-natured based people have fear as their counterpart. It is not until you really get converted that the fear of the Lord begins to operate because that happens through repentance. When you repent, you shift from the natural state to the "super-natural" state. That's where explanation loses its foothold because you just stepped out of the "First Adam" nature and into the "Second Adam" nature. That's where water turns to wine, crippled turns to leaping and dancing, dead turns to raised, blind turns to seeing, and mute turns to speaking. This is the miraculous dimension.

Rhodes, Dr. Ron. "MIRACLES - Has Science Disproved the Miracles Associated with Jesus Christ? - ChristianAnswers.net." *Christiananswers.net,* christiananswers.net/q-eden/rfsm-miracles.html.

CHAPTER 6

A miracle, by definition, is "an extraordinary event manifesting divine intervention in human affairs." That's a pretty minimal explanation. That's the way the earth perceives it.

Here is God's explanation of a miracle. In Luke chapter 1, the angel of the Lord shows up. Obviously, it was Gabriel who had the information from God that a child would be born and Mary would be the container with capacity to hold that child. He would become the redemptive child of Israel and deliver His people from their sins. And so, here comes the angel. Nobody else knows. He starts speaking into this atmosphere called earth. But he comes from the Throne of God, so now he's speaking a dialogue from heaven to earth, giving Mary throne room perception and astounding her to no end.

God tried it six months earlier with the same angel but with a different individual named Zacharias; but he kind of doubted. (After you've been in church a while, there is a tendency to doubt new dimensions.)

It's easier to doubt new dimensions because you think you know God. The thing I have practiced is never to think I know what is going to happen next. I have trained my brain to do that. I don't want to become so "Pentecostal" that I think I know more than God. If you remark, after hearing a message, "Well, I've heard that before," don't tell anybody that. You're letting them know God's having to tell you twice!

When I hear something, and then I hear it repeated, I pause.

I ask myself, "What am I not catching about this? Why is God bringing this to my attention again? What else is here that I missed the last time? I want to understand more of it."

Here is the problem that we have: when we get "settled" we don't like to explore. Most Americans don't like to explore because we've "got it." We are it. We believe that we are the world's "superpower." As Americans, in general, we are so arrogant and proud. As a country and a nation, we think we've got it all together—but, the reality is, we are really falling apart.

It is the nature of being settled. It's the "plateau" perception. When you get to the point where you've got everything you need, you feel like you really don't need anything. God forbid that we embrace that mentality. (It is easy to do since we are not suffering like other countries.)

When Brother Quintero from San Jose went to Venezuela, he gave a lady a twenty-dollar bill because God told him to. The lady collapsed on the floor in astonishment because the average wage there was one dollar a month. When she saw that twenty-dollar bill, she broke. She just couldn't take it. She began weeping and saying, "Why are you doing this?"

He said, "God told me to give this to you."

She said, "Do you realize, this is almost a year and a half of my earnings?"

So, we really don't understand. We cannot comprehend it because we use twenty bucks for fast food, so it's easy for us to get settled and plateaued. That's one of the most dangerous places to be because expectancy is for those who keep climbing. We can't afford to fall asleep. We've got to keep this expectancy level at a prime location because the supernatural never stops. It NEVER STOPS! We stop—it doesn't stop.

"Well, you know, God may do it, and He may not…"

When was the last time you climbed a 10,000-foot mountain in the Spirit? When was the last time you got that zealous?

When you had a need?

Or when you had a passion to explore?

We are missing a passion for exploration. Have you ever experienced a great Sunday service, with the Spirit of God moving? People go home or to a restaurant and have great fellowship; the next day they wake up, and they can't even remember what the preacher preached. (Sometimes the preacher himself can't even remember what he preached. I've had those Mondays too.)

Here's what God has been teaching me. He said, "When you wake up, remember, I opened a door, and no man can shut it." And I thought, "Wait a minute. If He opens a door and all I do is just walk through the door and stand there, do you know what I'm missing? EXPLORATION. I didn't explore!"

When the preacher preaches, a whole bunch of stuff is going to open up. When it opens up, your responsibility is not just to get the best you can out of what happened. The next day, when you wake up, that door is still open—that access point is still available. That room is still worthy of exploration. When you go home after a church meeting, it's not just about, "Wow, we had a great meeting!"

Instead, think about this: What did you take in your quiver? What did you take in your backpack that is now going to follow you back to your house? When you wake up on Monday, start worshiping the Lord and say, "God, I sensed something back there when I was in that meeting—when I was in that session—when I was in that move of the Holy Ghost. What else is in here? What is behind this door? What's behind this furniture? What's in this place? I'm going to peel it apart until I find every treasure, every jewel, every gift, and every calling that's in here!"

EXPLORE!

CHAPTER 7

Creative, or Reactionary?

Reactionary has no exploration built into it. Creative has all kinds of exploration built into it. When you feel creative, you're searching everything. Creative modes, by nature, make you want to explore.

God said, "I'm going to make my church creative because I want them to explore."

Romans 11:34-36 says:

"For who hath known the mind of the Lord? or who hath been his counselor? Or who hath first given to him, and it shall be recompensed unto him again? For of him, and through him, and to him, are …"

Most things? Some things?

"...ALL things to whom be glory for ever. Amen."

God said, "Look, I've got ALL things!"

You respond, "Well, why didn't you give them to me?"

He will say, "Because you didn't explore! I had ALL things built into this."

The Prophet Isaiah has a conniption going on in Isaiah chapter 5. (He's kind of reactionary here.) Isaiah has been affected by the earth, and he has been affected by his surroundings. He has become "reactionary" before God. Here is what he says in Isaiah 5:8 -

"Woe unto them that join house to house, that lay field to field, till there be no place, that they may be placed alone in the midst of the earth!"

He's kind of upset. Let's look at verse number eleven:

"Woe unto them that rise up early in the morning, that they may follow strong drink; that continue until night, till wine inflame them!"

He's frustrated at the actions of people who have been affected by hell. Don't ever let your ministry be a frustration because you can't get to somebody. Get into heavenly places, and God will give you a key. Doesn't God know how to reach every soul of man?

He won't cross their will—not yet. He will at Judgement. We are not taking our wills to Heaven. That's why we've got to practice giving it up while we are on earth; that's why we must "die," every day. We must practice giving up our will, because there aren't going to be two wills in Heaven. Someone tried that once and he got his name changed. (Not only did he get his will kicked out, but he got his name changed, from "Lucifer" to "satan.") I don't want that kind of name change. I'd rather go from "Jacob" to "Israel."

Watch what Isaiah says in verses 18-20:

"Woe unto them that draw iniquity with cords of vanity, and sin as it were with a cart rope:

That say, Let him make speed, and hasten his work, that we may see it: and let the counsel of the Holy One of Israel draw nigh and come, that we may know it!

Woe unto them that call evil good, and good evil; that put darkness for light, and light for darkness; that put bitter for sweet, and sweet for bitter!"

Do you know what that sounds like? It sounds like the internet. This sounds like the media, and preachers preaching off the media or the internet. They are getting their information from the conflict of earth instead of getting their information from the impartation of Heaven. So, they've become reactionary preachers trying to fix something.

Do you know what happens if you cut grass? You're not going to get rid of it; you're going to make it grow. That's why John the Baptist, preaching on repentance in Luke 3:9 and Matthew 3:10, said you need to lay the "axe to the ROOT."

It's kind of like chopping off a branch: all you've done is, you've pruned it! You haven't chopped the tree down–you've made it stronger. That's why people who try to get rid of their habits by only dealing with the habit instead of the root, end up having worse problems.

They're just cutting the grass. They come every Sunday, they come once a week, and they're just "cutting the grass."

They say, "Oh, I feel so much better," but they feel better because the grass looks pretty. They didn't handle the root, and the problem will only grow worse.

Let's continue reading in Isaiah chapter 5:21-23:

"Woe unto them that are wise in their own eyes, and prudent in their own sight!

Woe unto them that are mighty to drink wine, and men of strength to mingle strong drink:

Which justify the wicked for reward, and take away the righteousness of the righteous from him!"

It seems like you can almost get a picture of God. God's just letting Isaiah talk, thinking, "Are you done yet? There's something else I wanted to show you, and you're so stuck on 'woes' that I can't show you the real 'WOAH.' I'm sitting up here on a throne."

So, we finally get to the sixth chapter. (We know there were not originally chapters and verses, so this is a single writing.)

Isaiah 6:1 says:

"In the year that king Uzziah died I saw also the Lord sitting upon a throne, high and lifted up, and his train filled the temple."

Until whatever is "king" in your life dies, you can't see what's perhaps right in front of you.

What is "king" in your life? Whatever you talk about the most and whatever your conversation is mostly revolved around. If you're not talking about God when you get to church, you're probably not talking about God when you leave church.

I've listened to people talking in the foyer before a church service, and I've thought, "Man, they're not ready for church. It's going to take us 30 minutes to start. They're going to have to sing just to get people's minds in the building, and then, church will start when they hand me the mic!" We've been through that several times, haven't we?

I had one pastor tell me, "Well, do what you can."

I thought, "Do what I can?" I didn't tell the people that. I spared them.

God did move, although it took a while. It was closer to the end that He moved—but it's closer to the *end*, and He is moving!

Finally, Isaiah noticed; God finally got Isaiah's attention off the reactionary. He got his attention on the creative, and Isaiah said, "I saw also the Lord, sitting upon a throne…"

Well, you can't see that from earth's perspective. You've got to get into a different dimension to see that. Isaiah stopped seeing the drunkard. He stopped seeing the busybody. He stopped seeing the self-righteous. He stopped seeing all the stuff that was affecting him and attained another view. He got a little higher and broke through, now at a place where he could see clearly.

God said, "Let me show you what's been here the whole time. It's not that it wasn't here—it's just that you had your focus somewhere else, and you couldn't see it by reason of what you were focused on."

Then Isaiah saw it: angels with six wings, flying with covered faces and feet.

Isaiah 6:2-3 says:

"Above it stood the seraphims: each one had six wings; with twain he covered his face, and with twain he covered his feet, and with twain he did fly.

And one cried unto another, and said, 'Holy, holy, holy, is the Lord of hosts: the whole earth is full of his glory.'"

It's interesting. If you look at the parallel of the books of Isaiah and Revelation, the same throne, same angels, and same setting is mentioned in both books. But John sees more than Isaiah because the time is different. The closer we get to the end of time, the more God is going to allow us to start seeing. Those angels in Revelation don't have their eyes covered. You can see their eyes. This is huge because we are now at the end of time, and God's going to start opening the eyes of the church like He has never done before.

CHAPTER 8

Think about this: Revelation addresses the seven churches and says, "He that hath an ear, let him hear…". Why is God so intent on everybody being able to hear, in the church? It makes a lot of sense. You see, God is causing the world to start hearing.

The end-time is going to require a church that can hear very clearly because we will need to be ahead of the game. Wasn't it the centurion soldier, standing by the cross, who perceived that Jesus was God manifested in the flesh? While everybody was looking at what was dying, he perceived, in Mark 15:39, "…Truly this man was the Son of God."

Don't say that God isn't talking to those in the world. This is a signal that the church needs to hear better than it's ever heard before. How are we going to do that if we are not in heavenly places? It's much easier to hear from God if we are sitting near one another than if I'm down here struggling with some battle from hell that has my attention and has befuddled me. What if I become so entangled in warfare that I can't pay attention to the Word of the Lord?

The fact is: God is trying to get us to ask the question before we engage the sword.

What got Peter in trouble? He drew his sword before he asked a question.

What got Israel in trouble? They drew their sword before they ever inquired of the Lord. When they didn't inquire of the Lord, that's when they were defeated; they lost a lot of men during those times. They would not inquire of the Lord.

The Lord did not give them permission to go fight. They just figured they could. And you know what? We can. We have the power of the Holy Ghost. We have the dominion of the Spirit of the Lord that is in us, called the Holy Ghost. We have the Blood of the Lamb. We have weapons for warfare because our warfare is not carnal. We know it is "... mighty through God to the pulling down of strong holds" (2 Corinthians 10:4).

And just because we CAN doesn't mean we SHOULD!

We have a natural thought process that says, "Hey—I'm going to win!" Because we CAN. That's the one thing we are sure of—that we can win. For, (as the song goes) "No matter what the weapon is, I want you to know that I win!" We get all excited over kicking the devil's hide, but do we really have permission for that particular battle? Isn't it better to ask that question?

I perceive that people have been wiped out in warfare because they actually didn't have permission, and they took it upon themselves to make the choice.

Do you know what that draw into warfare was? It was just a distraction. And, God was saying, "I don't want you to deal with that. I've got something else I want to show you." And all the while we were drawn into wasting our time, dealing with something that wasn't even our battle in the first place. For the battle is the Lord's. I repeat, the battle is NOT yours, it is the LORD'S.

God says, "Put your focus on ME! I'm not interested in the enemy. I know you can wipe him out. I gave you the tools to do so–and every now and then, you're going to have to do that."

Here's what I noticed: there's something very interesting about celestial places where the creative starts working. When God changed a city, how did He do it? He didn't rebuke devils. He didn't take dominion over the town so there could be a great harvest. I've heard that teaching, and I understand the point behind it, but think about this: where is the biblical reference where Jesus taught us how to win a city? The Gadarenes is the biblical reference. That's how you win a city. That's a city that had no God-consciousness. They didn't want Jesus to stay after he healed that demoniac; they sent him home. "Get out of here," they said, "Go back!"

The Lord says, "Don't worry, I'll handle the spirit world."

When the man wanted to go with them, the Lord said, "No, no, no. I put a miracle inside of you and this miracle is going to multiply. So, here's what I'd like you to do. You stay, and you go publish what great things the Lord has done for you." So Jesus put a miracle inside of him, delivered him, and said, "This miracle has multiplication built into it."

Now, I don't see any stories about rebuking devils. I don't see any stories about having prayer meetings, engaging in warfare, or trying to get rid of hell and pushing it back. No.

The only reason you rebuke hell is when it is attached to somebody. That's when Jesus rebuked the spirits—when they were attached to the man. But when Jesus was trying to take over a city, He didn't do that. He sent the man into the city with a testimony and with the miraculous because the man had a MIRACLE!

If you study that story and study that miracle, the word, "publish," in its extended, Grecian translation, actually means, "casting down spirits" or "declaring His victory to fallen spirits." That's what the word, "published," means. It means "Declaring His victory," not yours. When you get a miracle, it's not your victory—it's the Lord's! When God heals me, that's not my victory. I just get to enjoy it. It's actually *His* victory.

So, what the Lord was telling that man was, "Look, I put my victory inside of you. Now that you have my victory inside of you, every time you open your mouth, it's going to loose my victory inside of that city. My victory, by default, will push back the spirit world."

That's the reason why death, hell, and the grave were conquered—that's the victory of the Lord! That's the greatest victory that exists. That's why the redemptive plan has so much power to push back evil spirits. When somebody gets a miracle and they get a "God-Victory," that victory pushes back spirits.

"And he [the man who was delivered] departed, and began to publish in Decapolis how great things Jesus had done for him: and all men did marvel" (Mark 5:20).

Gadara was just one city in the midst of the Decapolis, which was a region of ten cities. So, an entire region was shaken because one man had a miracle that pushed back the spirits of hell.

CHAPTER 9

What dimensions?

Think about the Moses law that was established on Mt. Sinai, where Moses set a line, and wherever Moses set the line of the mountain, that's where the mountain started. Nobody could cross it, and that's the way it was from that point forward.

So, the Israelites adopted this concept: "Don't touch the presence. Don't touch the Holy of Holies—the atmosphere." Think about it.

Read through Matthew, Mark, Luke, and John. Read through all of those stories until you get to the woman with the "issue of blood." Prior to that moment, nobody touched the hem of his garment. They desired to touch Him, but nobody ever did. He always touched them.

But watch this: He pushed the spirits back through a miracle and a testimony, and a publishing in the land. Then, He brought in the next dimension—God multiplied the miracles. He had the liberty to speak doctrine (because you can't speak doctrine until you have somebody's attention).

People get it backwards! Why are we trying to get people in the church from the head to the soul instead of from the soul to the head? That's the backwards approach. We teach 50,000 Bible studies, and 1,000 people come in. That's a bad ratio. That ratio just bothers me. Doesn't it bother you?

I'm thinking, "God, is it really this hard? You didn't seem to make it this hard. Why are we having so much trouble? Help us, Lord! We need your help!"

God started talking to me. He said, "How do you worship God?"

He said, "I taught you how you're supposed to worship God. Worship the Lord with all of your heart, all of your soul, mind, and strength." The word "mind" is toward the end—not at the beginning. But we're trying to convince them. Here's the problem: If you convince them to come in, something can convince them to get out.

But, if they have a supernatural deliverance, they get a miracle, and they come in by reason of supernatural movement, when are they going to leave? They aren't going to leave because their hearts will say, "This is where God healed me of cancer."

"This is where God opened my blind eyes."

"This is where God stretched my leg out!"

So, Jesus walked into the city, and the woman with an issue of blood thought, "If I may just touch the hem of His garment, I will be made whole."

Think about it—she touched the hem of His garment and was healed, Jairus' daughter got raised from the dead, and it's a "cool deal." Miracles broke out. It was a phenomenal platform that had opened up.

But think about this: later, in Mark chapter six, Jesus sends them in the boat across the Sea of Galilee a second time. This is the story where He is going to go up to pray on the mountain. During the fourth watch of the night, He comes to the disciples' aid walking on the water. They end up landing in Gennesaret, in the Northwestern region. The woman with the issue of blood resided nearby, so by now, word had gotten out, "If you just touch His hem, you will be healed!"

"And when they were gone over, they came into the land of Gennesaret. And when the men of that place had knowledge of him, they sent out into all that country round about, and brought unto him all that were diseased; and besought him that they might only touch the hem of his garment: and as many as touched were made perfectly whole" (Matthew 14:34-36).

Nobody ever thought of this before. This is brand new. This is like headline news—and it has gone throughout the region. They didn't have cell phones, telephones, fax machines, or any of that stuff. They had word of mouth. So, apparently, the word had spread from village to village and the word had spread by mouth. Word of mouth is still the greatest form of advertising to this day because it's publishing something. It's creating an atmosphere.

So, this concept has now been shared from village to village.

"Hey! Did you hear? She just touched His HEM, and she was made whole!"

"Really? Well, no, I hadn't heard!"

"Well, my friend was there. Then he told my other friend, who told my other friend…"

It's like the game of telephone on steroids.

When Jesus calmed the storm, it was calmed without words. He never spoke to that storm because when you get into higher dimensions, you use fewer words.

That's why the handkerchief dimension is one of the highest dimensions. When the sons of Sceva went to try and cast demons out of the man, Paul was not on location and Jesus was not on location. Still, those evil spirits looked at the sons of Sceva and said, "Hey! Jesus we know, and Paul we know…" Paul was not even on location. It was just his cloth! His anointing was so powerful that it literally saturated the cloth so much that the devil recognized it.

CHAPTER 10

Dimensions without words: Jesus stepped into the boat with Peter after walking on water. They just stepped into that boat, and the storm said, "I'm not waiting for words." Immediately, the waves and the wind ceased to batter the ship. But Jesus never spoke to the storm; He only talked to Peter.

God is saying, "I'm trying to turn your attention away from the storm. The first time I had to deal with the storm myself because your focus was on it. This time, I dealt with the supernatural because your focus started to turn toward me–but then, you thought I was a devil."

The disciples cried out, "It is a GHOST!" when they saw Jesus. They weren't thinking "Casper" here. They screamed in fear, terribly afraid of the supernatural. It was the fourth watch of the night, which is also the last dimension of the era of time in the church.

God is about to launch this church into the supernatural, and we need to get comfortable with it. That's what God is trying to get the church to do–get accustomed to the supernatural. So, He's going to start having things show up to change the concepts of the church.

When our attention is drawn away from the enemy, then we can become acclimated to God's supernatural movements. In John's writing, the boat immediately arrived at the shore. I realized, "Wow! The boat got translated!"

"Then they willingly received him into the ship, and immediately the ship was at the land whither they went" (John 6:21).

You may be thinking, "Well, I don't know if that happened–if the boat was translated."

You can believe what you want to—but that's what I believe. I believe we're getting into dimensions where–it's not just one or two people—it's the whole boat! It's an immediate translation.

So, Jesus walked on the water, got into the disciples' boat, calmed that storm, and showed up at the shore. The Bible says, in that writing, after they got off the boat, that everyone who touched His hem was healed. I thought, "Where did those people get that from?"

They could have only gotten this idea from one place: the village where the woman touched His hem. It had spread so wide that everyone in the Northwest region and those who showed up said, "Hey—He's coming! If you'll just touch the hem, it will heal you! There's something in Him."

It created an atmosphere, just like people have created an atmosphere to destroy the devil, which has become popular to the point that it has permeated our music.

Think about the songs we sing. For instance, think about the song that says, "I give you glory. I give you praise. Because my enemy did not triumph."

You're excited because the devil didn't win? Think about the words we are actually singing. I know I defraud the whole youth group when I talk about that.

But think about what's propagated. The devil has the earth's attention because there's been something loosed in the Heavens. He is trying to keep people from the perception of what's loosed in the Heavens.

Here's my whole concept behind teaching this way: Isaiah 46 talks about a statement that we use quite often, that God knows "the end from the beginning."

Isaiah 46:10 NKJV

"Declaring the end from the beginning,
And from ancient times things that are not yet done,
Saying, 'My counsel shall stand,
And I will do all My pleasure,'"

Isaiah 46:10 ESV

"Who announces the end from the beginning
and reveals beforehand what has not yet occurred;
who says, 'My plan will be realized,
I will accomplish what I desire,'"

The end from the beginning? That means He has to loose the answer before you have the problem. That means that He would have to loose the miracle before you ever had the crisis.

So that means, before you ever get into a trial, God has already released a solution.

CHAPTER 11

So, what is required of us to attain this understanding? Alignment. We've got to get in the vein! The devil starts reacting because the creative just got loosed. When I step into a battle, the devil will say, "Oh no! If he pays attention to what just got released in the atmosphere, then something is going to happen in his world that cannot be overtaken by our world!"

So, here's what I would suggest—not "if" you get attacked but "when" you get attacked.

When I got attacked recently, I didn't address it. I didn't say anything. I didn't ask God to handle it. I didn't even pull out an offering. I was still in my pajamas. I was sitting in a chair, and I thought, "I'm not going to say anything. I'm not going to do anything. I'm just going to put my attention on you, oh Lord."

And God began to talk to me. He said, "Remember: Creative or reactionary." I said, "Yes, Sir. You've created something—because there's a reaction."

I wonder how many of you have recently been under reactionary attack.

Remember, something has gotten loosed on your behalf.

God has heard your prayer. God has witnessed your faith. God has seen your tears. He has listened as you have petitioned Him. He has heard you ask, and He has responded. The attack has nothing to do with the devil's ability. It has to do with how he's reacting to Heaven's response to your original prayer request.

Hell is not a resistance; it's a reaction.

I'll repeat it once more: hell is NOT a resistance. It's a reaction!

The moment you calculate hell as a resistance, you treat it differently. The moment you calculate it as a reaction, you treat it differently.

Did you always respond to your kids when they reacted? No, because you "learned" them. You realized that they were just trying to get something. It's a reaction because they think they're going to get "this" if they act like "that."

But kids also "learn" us!

Do you think hell doesn't know humanity or its physical structure? It has been studying humanity for over 6,000 years. Hell knows body language! Body language is repetitive because everything under the sun is repetitive. Everything above the sun is new. That's why the Bible says in Ecclesiastes 1:9 (CEB), "There's nothing new under the sun."

It doesn't say there's nothing new above the sun because all things that are new are above the sun. That's where God is. That's creative!

That's why the Bible talks about a "new heaven and a new earth." That's why it talks about a "new Jerusalem." All those things are conceived out of creative settings—a heavenly atmosphere. So, when you get into God's world and God gives you a Word of instruction, revival accompanies that Word.

However, if a certain method is preached across the church, at large, and each local congregation tries to adopt it as a set program, it usually doesn't work. This happens when people focus on a method rather than the creative flow of God's Spirit.

In other words, that particular instruction given by a man of God may have been God's creative moment for one congregation, but it may not be the same method God wants to use with every church (e.g. if a minister receives a revelation about witnessing at his/her church, that method may not be as effective in another church at a different spiritual state). Sometimes there is a creative Word given to a specific church in a "God moment" by a man or woman of God, and we reach to grab their Word instead of seeking God for our own.

Don't take that one method as a "motto" for your church. Just be aware that, if God gave the preacher a revelation, we should attempt to get to where he/she was when they received the revelation.

Then, ask God for a personalized Word for our church, ministry, or family. Let the personal Word metabolize and work meticulously as a resource.

How do you have revival? Get into God's world! God knows how to have revival. He knows how to draw souls in accordance with His Word.

"And I, if I be lifted up from the earth, will draw all men unto me" (John 12:32).

The Lord says, "Let me show you what my signal to myself was. I'll come down, I'll get a body, I'll let it die on a cross, and it will bring such attention to me that they won't even notice that hell is moving."

Jesus got a Roman soldier's attention. How hard is that to do? That centurion was responsible for one hundred soldiers, at least; nevertheless, God was able to get the attention of somebody who was meticulously trained as an officer of the ancient Roman army. The centurion was able to take his attention off his duty and notice what was moving in the Spirit—and key into it.

Whether you're standing next to a cross—or working as a bank teller—it's kind of the same. God can take that dimension of the natural off the one He is reaching–just for a second–and they can hear.

God is beginning to quicken people who are not even in the church yet and will begin to use them to provide financial flows, based on the scripture that says, "...shall men give into your bosom..." (Luke 6:38). The blessings are going to start coming from people around us.

As we come to a conclusion, lift your hands where you are (if you are able) and begin to talk to God. Your atmosphere is carrying an opening for people—who don't know how to hear God—to start hearing the voice of the Spirit; it will be the introductory process for them to get miracles, signs, and wonders, so they can be drawn unto the Lord Jesus Christ—and by supernatural activity.

Follow along with this prayer:

Lord, by the authority of the Word of God, You attach these motions and notions upon us in this hour.

Lord, what You have articulated by Word, by Spirit, by deed, and by atmosphere, let it be loosed and now begin to metabolize.

We ask that God would begin to now cause the creative dimension to become common speech— the creative dimension to become common function—the creative dimension to enter churches, to enter families, to enter lives, to enter ministries, to enter jobs, and to enter atmospheres in the name of the Lord Jesus Christ.

By the authority of the Word of God, I loose the creative in the name of Jesus. I loose the manifested works of God to come forth out of your hands, out of your mouth, out of your eyes, out of your soul, and out of your being.

On this day that You have created, cause some to cross the line from the reactionary to the creative. In the name of Jesus!

SPECIAL THANKS

Special thanks to our dear friend, Donna Ten Eyck. Thank you for the many hours of reading, editing, and discussing the concepts in this message, working with us, making sure that this book rang true to the integrity of the word spoken through Brother Eli Hernandez. We also thank you for your many years of faithful friendship and prayer support, even up until Eli Hernandez' eternal home-going. May the Lord continue to bless your powerful ministry and bless your life.

We extend our thanks to the following ministers who also helped us with content editing for this work: Pastor Mike Mendenhall, Rev. Jeffrey E. Brickle, Ph.D., Pastor Randy Blizzard, and Rev. Alex Leon. Thank you for taking the time out of your busy schedules to take this project to heart and suggest changes that made this manuscript read all the better.

Thank you, Moriah Sachs, for your excellent help with the final proof editing for this book. And thank you, Charity Hernandez, for your help with the graphic design for this project. Both of you have been a tremendous help and this book would not have been completed without the kind sacrifice of your time and talents.

We give special honor to Rev. Gordon Winslow for his contribution of writing the Foreword for this book. We are grateful beyond words, as he wrote for us in the midst of his own storm. He was a great friend to Eli Hernandez. Our prayers go out to his family and all those who were impacted by his powerful ministry.

Thank you, Pastor Nonoy Lachica, for providing the sound recording of the message, "Creative or Reactionary." Thank you for hosting the conference that launched this heavenly message; may God's blessings be upon you and Spirit & Truth Lighthouse.

Finally, we extend our very special thanks to everyone who contributed an endorsement for this book. We love and appreciate all of you, and we thank the Lord for your friendships which greatly delighted the heart of Brother Eli Hernandez. Each and every one of you held a special place in his life and ministry. Thank you for taking the time to read this work and write from your hearts, that others would be encouraged to read and glean also. May the Lord continue to bless you all.

ABOUT THE AUTHOR

Eli Hernandez was an international evangelist. Born in San Jose, California, in 1960, he was called into the ministry by the Spirit of God at a very young age. Though his life took many turns in his teenage and young adult years, he finally acknowledged his call into the ministry in his early twenties.

He met his wife, Kathy, while working in the city of Boston. They married in 1984 and later moved to Houston, Texas, where Eli and Kathy Hernandez worked as youth ministers from 1986 until 1989. From there, the Lord called him into full-time ministry as an evangelist; for the next thirty years, Eli and Kathy Hernandez traveled across the United States and the world, preaching the Good News of the Gospel, promoting God's amazing power, and witnessing great miracles and healings, Holy Ghost in-fillings, and powerful manifestations of God's Spirit wherever they ministered.

In 2016, Eli and Kathy Hernandez, and their daughter, Charity, moved to Las Vegas, Nevada, from where they continued to launch their ministry. In 2020, while traveling, Eli Hernandez contracted COVID-19. After 45 days on the ventilator and under full sedation in the VA Hospital, Brother Hernandez left this life for his eternal reward. He is greatly missed by countless numbers of people—yet his ministry continues to bless people through his writings and through the messages that he preached—many still available on the internet.

A documentary on his life, entitled, "Man of God: Eli Hernandez," is available on YouTube and on the ministry website: **revivalinprogress.com**

Other works by Eli Hernandez include the books, "Maintaining Divine Operation" and "A World Beyond the Stars," (both also available in Spanish) and a music therapy project entitled, "Healing Overtures for Physical Enhancement" (HOPE)—along with other instrumental music projects. These works may be found on Amazon and on the website, revivalinprogress.com.

Made in the USA
Coppell, TX
14 January 2026

69148290R00036